INFINITE ME

AASTIK GAUR

Copyright © Aastik Gaur
All Rights Reserved.

This book has been published with all efforts taken to make the material error-free after the consent of the author. However, the author and the publisher do not assume and hereby disclaim any liability to any party for any loss, damage, or disruption caused by errors or omissions, whether such errors or omissions result from negligence, accident, or any other cause.

While every effort has been made to avoid any mistake or omission, this publication is being sold on the condition and understanding that neither the author nor the publishers or printers would be liable in any manner to any person by reason of any mistake or omission in this publication or for any action taken or omitted to be taken or advice rendered or accepted on the basis of this work. For any defect in printing or binding the publishers will be liable only to replace the defective copy by another copy of this work then available.

Dedicated to my parents who have always supported and inspired me.

Contents

Acknowledgements

I wish to acknowledge and show my gratitude towards one and all who in some way, have inspired me to jot this book down. God's blessings make for a great start and I worship my parents, hence I foremost wish to thank them and send them lots of love.

I also wanna thank all my friends, family, mentors and even strangers who at some point in life helped me go on with my dreams. A special thanks to my english teachers who supported me when I used to share with them a little writeup with broken grammar or incorrect words.

Lastly, I wish to express my gratitude towards the modern day resources which allowed me to publish the book hassle-free. Thanks to everyone who ever believed in me.

1. Back To My First

A young boy,
Mere 9 in age,
I sat on my bed,
With a blank page,
Sachin! Sachin!
Spoke my mind,
For the very first time,
I wrote a rhyme,
Competitive to the utmost,
Full of zest like my mom,
Creativity filled inside,
And yet a life so norm,
Motherhood and memories,
They share a bond so weird,
I will grow up too fast,
Maybe that's what my mom feared,
So, she played with me,
She explored me as I did my life,
Making origami, greeting cards,
Unaware, I used to cause strife,
And I sat that day,
My mom right beside me,
Going through a Talent-Hunt booklet,
Trying to guide me,

And somewhere in that blank page,
I was completely lost,
Somewhere in that little rhyme,
I started to find myself,
A young boy,
Much more than just flesh,
That's when it all started,
10 years later I'm writing this afresh.

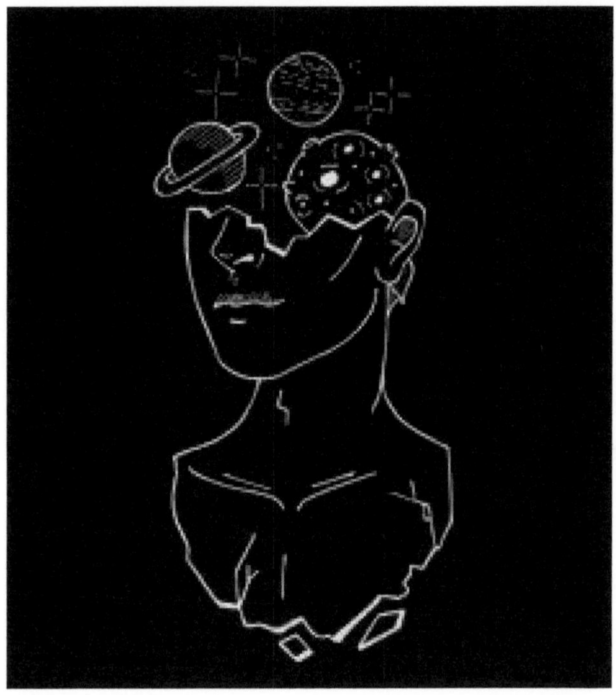

2. Boarded Up

It's surprising how we sapiens tend to be,
It's surprising,
What millions of neurons can do,
With an ounce of dopamine or adrenaline,
Behold, behold for you are thy only master,
Your own slave though you be,
Its October already,
The Fall has begun,
The old redwood miles into the deep dark forest,
Has started shedding its leaves,
And yet, when nature itself is keen to let go,
We sapiens,
We are holding back,
Resisting change like ever before,
Realising how easy it could be,
But we are never finished with our chores,
Educating young generations,
That its merely a chemical heart,
Little do we know about the stranded ideas,
Which lie buried beneath us as we ignore the art,
Caught up in illusions,
Living on lies,
Believing in the non-existant,
Keeping secrets from even the skies,

October 5th twenty-ten,
I saw that creaking shack in the countryside,
An aged man 'boarding up' its windows,
Preparing for the racing storm cause he has nowhere else to hide,
I guess now I understand,
We sapiens,
Why we have masquerades on,
Living alone in a world of millions,
How we are stuck in the memories,
As we struggle to move on,
I guess,
I guess I know,
That I'm doing the same,
Lying without no shame,
When I tell my sister "It'll be alright,
Its just a chemical heart".,
And yet,
I cry alone in the shower,
And then I claim to be smart?
No, no we're no different,
We're the shacks in the living world,
Boarding up to take the hits,
To endure the pain life has to give.
Peace out!

3. One Fine Day

"Swish, swish, swish,"
The crisp pages of your book will rustle,
The dandelions, ballerinas of the balcony,
You'd take a sip of tea,
And hum along to the songs of old,
You'll breathe a little deeper,
And you'll smile,

One day,
One fine day.

The album you hold so dear,
Soaked in the elixir of love,
For now, put it in the cupboard.
Cause one day, you'll take it out,
You'll watch 'Maya' point me out,
She'd go, "Look, its daddy!"
You'll caress her hair,
You'll breathe a little deeper,
And you'll smile.

One day,
One fine day,

The moments you hold so dear,

The memories which are flooding your mind,
For now, push them away,
Cause one day you'll miss me,
You'll wish if only you could kiss me,
You'll order 'chole bhatoore',
Our occasional love,
Then you'll breathe a little deeper,
And you'll smile,

One day,
One fine day,

For now, know that I'm gone,
Cause one day the radio will play "Ek Ajnabee"
You'll close your eyes and feel my presence,
And you'll breathe a little deeper,
And you'll smile,

One day,
One fine day.

Henn Kim

4. Be My Voice

I've seen people shout,
Great men are the ones who make history,
But today I write about,
The girl who was lost in a known mystery,
With a heart as weak as short she'd dress,
A voice as soft as the makeup she wore,
Pathetic! I witnessed, 'great men' in the press,
Said, 'Law is apex, can't say no more.'
Added those 'men', with a feeling so holy,
'Sorry for the loss', in a voice so lowly,
Grew up as an orphan, her eyes had a zest,
She sprinted to the woods, and stopped for no rest,
Halted in a city, a kingdom of gold,
For hands so tiny, this was too much to hold,
Coated with tats,
With knowledge so little,
Had dinner with the rats,
That body so brittle,
And she mused,
About the mother who left her on a road,
And the father, mumbling, 'Was I a load?'
And she wept,
With paining legs she crept,
She had just a rag for her beauty, to cover,
The blood on her face, red makeup by a 'lover',

Raped by a beast,
Murdered by choice,
Died in a crowd,
Uttering,
'Will you be my voice?'.

5. A Burning Room

Love as in its evilest forms,
Slow dancing in a burning room,
Eyes closed as I savor your presence,
Toxic desires of a pleasing doom,

Tied up in your manipulative hinges,
Is it ok if a little longer I stay?
I'll tolerate all your darkest parts,
As long as you promise to never go away,

Show me the roughest of your love,
Take me in your arms,
I'm broken already, now I love the pain,
Cause I'm in love with your charms,

I choke on my own sobs,
I can't breathe but I try,
I might be a masochist,
But with pain I cry,

I 've run out of hopes,
But I know I deserve better,
To let go will be as worse,
Another heartbreak, another burnt letter,

Be here in any of the ways you can,
Don't leave me by myself though,
Kiss me like its the last of your love,
Or hurt me enough to make me go,

Love is foreign to you,
So is purpose in my life,
If I don't one day kill myself,
Maybe I could be your wife,

Or you could keep me close,
Just the way we are,
I could let you break me a little more,
But please don't ever go far.

Love as in its evilest forms,
Slow dancing in a burning room,
Eyes closed as I savor your presence,
Toxic desires of a pleasing doom.

6. My Mother

My mother, she is different from all,
She is a writer with no love for words,
A poetess whose poems are like glass to the birds,
Confused, I know, you try to understand,
No words, no poems? Like a mirage in the sand,
She wrote a story with her heart,
Not with ink, but with love from every part,
She wrote me,
Wrote me with happiness and love,
With unshown struggles but a smile above,
She wrote me,
Dedicated, focused, to shape me her best,
Played, fought, cried, never had a rest,
She composed me,
With rhythm, with beauty,
Out of want, not just duty,
She carved me,
Like wonders made out of wood,
As nice as I try to be good,
She gave me, hidden powers with the tone,
Made me such, I can stand on my own,
Yes, she is the author, the poetess,
Of the story and the poem I happen to be.

7. Hey Beautiful

Hey beautiful,
You, yes you!
Am I the first to say that?
Or you're scared to believe?

After you take a shower,
Stand in front of the mirror,
Naked!
Do you look straight,
Or your head bows down?

Its ok, you can trust me,
Show me that deep-hidden terror,
Crooked!
That smile you hate?
How'd you lose your crown?

I'll touch you,
With the tip of my fingers,
Or a gentle kiss,
I'll slide my fingers on your skin,
You'll feel it embed in your soul,

Is that forehead too large?
I could kiss it,

More kisses for you,
Are those eyes not your favorite color?
I'll stare at them for hours,
More like drown deep inside the love they reflect,

Does that nose feel like an outcast?
I'd pinch it and shake your head,
Then tickle you and run out,
What about the lips?
Are they imperfect?
I'd kiss them passionately,
In a way you'll remember,

Are you afraid to tilt your head?
I'll slide a fingertip on your neck,
Or place a gentle peck on your shoulder,
Does the size of your breasts bother you?
I'd pinch your nipples,
And watch them get perky under my hands,

I'll rub that grown belly,
Just the way you like,
I'll hold that waist,
And keep you close,
The fingers you consider too long,
I'll entangle them with mine,

Those hips which make you insecure,
I'd spank them gently while you make tea,

And then I'll enjoy hearing you frown,

The freckles on your cheek,
The wrinkles right below your eyes,
The childhood scars on your knees and elbows,
Or the shivering body,
With the touch of any guy,

I could love them,
Without no end,
I could admire you,
Along with your scars,
I could dream about you,
You don't even know how perfect you are,

So let them tell you,
How your body isn't fit for ideal,
You'll be the goddess of beauty,
In my own little heart-town,

Hey love!
You're beautiful!
I'd tell you when you turn 70,
White hair, brittle body,
I hope you smile at me,
With love but majorly with pride!

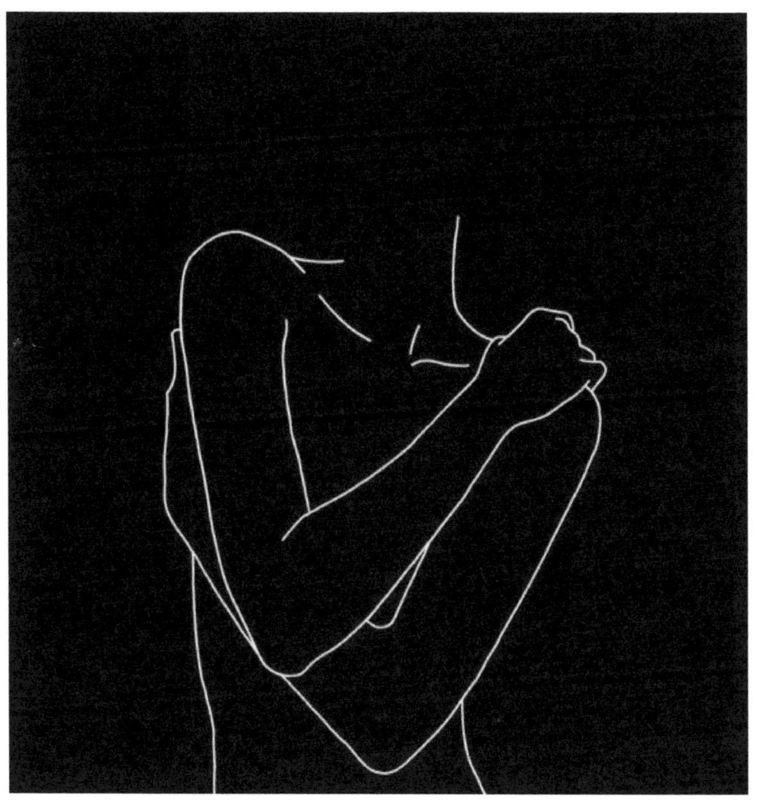

8. The Bud

So rough was the rain,
As if heaven was crying,
Heavy drops on soft petals,
Thunder clapped as the beauty was dying,
The artistic, tiny flower,
Once danced in the drizzle,
At times, swayed with the light breeze,
But the new bud was still in a puzzle,
How the music of the rain became a noise,
How the shower of love became a painful poise,
The bud, she saw the flower fall to rest,
She saw the raindrop hit her mother's chest,
The red elixir of life splattered on her face,
In moments, the sky was quite,
The wind had gone, painting the walls red from white,
She still still bloomed amidst the rubble and whither,
Memories of the storm had again now hit her,
It wasn't the music of her brother's videogame,
It was guns and rifles, from where the noise had came,
There were no clouds for the drought hit lands,
Massacred for no good, by monstrous hands,
Deep inside the flowery form she knew,
Lives of millions were in pathetic hands of few,
No food to eat, no water to drink,
Hours in the bunker she'd think,

How cruel is the war out there?!,
Boom!! Came a huge blast,
And she vanished in a blink.

9. Noah's Ark

His pen bleeds,
It jots the emotions inside his head,
Today, when he is scared he's falling,
I wish his pen could have said..

Its funny for he is blank and inkless,
For the same reasons he writes for and you have read,

He's an optimist,
With a constructive mind,
With an innocent soul,
And just a little too kind..

Sacrificing himself,
He's only left with a pieces few,
Scared to be alone,
Scared to lose them too,

What good is a man without a heart,
Yet he chose to give it up part by part,
Proud for the life he lives,
But isn't it too much, the hurt it gives?

He surrounds himself with vibes which keep him happy,
Today he is sulking in a place a little dark,

Flooded with pain, agony and loneliness,
Waiting for a Noah's Ark.

10. Love Is An Art

"Tera mujhse hai pehle ka naata koi.....", I sang,
Out of sync tune,
No melody in the voice,
Forgetting the lyrics,
Hush, one hell of a song choice..

" ....yun hi nhi dil lubhata koi ", I finished,
Nervous, anxious, worried,
Well it was worth a try,
You just gazed at me, smiling,
I looked away, too shy,

Isn't love surprising,
Makes you sing your heart out,
Only literally this time,
For a while you run out of words,
Heartbeats synced, as if a rhyme,

Sometimes it's the opposite,
You speak so much,
And yet it doesn't make sense,
Mixed emotions they say,
You're so serene and yet so tense,

Love is a mystery,

The kind of love this heart shares,
Its clearer than the sunny sky,
And yet somehow it scares,

You loved yourself,
And I loved to see,
And yet every time,
I just wanted it to be me,

Love is an art,
We're more than artists with a zest,
Lets paint together with our passions,
Cause our love-ly talent is the best.

11. A Sonnet To Them

Content with his content, he works with a zest,
Adventurous in ways, he is always in for a shot,
The boldness she caries, its way too hot,
She is willing to fly, she flies higher than the rest,

Unique and outstanding, she believes she can be the best,
There is a mystery to this guy, but a charm he has got,
Dreamy and optimistic, he's supportive, like a lot,
He is as fine as the wine served after a rich fest,

With the purest of all hearts, she is an inspiration to live,
High on humor, he spreads smiles like a sizzle,
She has a rhythm to her soul, her life is a song,

As innocent as a child, she has loads of love to give,
With a pint of mischief, she loves dancing in the drizzle,
There's genius to his wit, but his silence makes him strong.

12. Polaroids

In an era of fast and simple,
I wanna be complex and deep,
I'm sane,
But I crave for adventure,
I crave for love,
But the one which is hard to forget,

In a time of hidden chats,
And secured phones,
I wanna take risks,
I wanna have a box of polaroids,
Of you and me dancing,
Or the day I first hug you,
And I wanna hide it under my bed.

So long,
Since I've lived or loved,
In an era of obsession and addiction,
I wish to have memories,
Not to latch on to them one day,
But to look back and smile,

How often do we make memories?
The day you felt so loved that you teared up?
The night we talked for hours but it felt way more alive?

The day you were at the edge of giving up but you held my hand and stepped back?

I wanna capture those moments,
Not in my heart or mind,
Cause you see,
Situations change the way you feel,
But I wanna capture them yet,
Paint them on a canvas maybe,
Jot them down on the last page of my diary,
Click a polaroid and paste it on the cupboard,

Not to look at them and cry,
But to know how lucky and happy I felt for a while.

Love,
As they say,
Is neither evil nor sane,
It only exists and it stays.
Love isn't in the air,
Its in people and places.
Its in those polaroids,
Hidden under my bed.

13. From A Life Before

Saw you first in a random stalking,
And I felt relieved,
And I thought that you don't like talking,
Never waited for a fight before,

Made friends with a person common,
Judged you for your pride,
Showed me pieces that my life had missing,
Felt like you and me were getting close,

Told you things that I kept on thinking,
You made me feel so calm,
Both our lives were at same place sinking,
Knew your thorns and I called you rose,

Love ain't harsh but we had to suffer,
A couple hearts being alone,
Messed up and I made my life tougher,
Letting go of my scars you chose,

All along it was you, I wasn't looking,
Then one day I realized,
I could feel a little storm was cooking,
I had secrets and you asked me those,

All I wrote was a bad confession,
At a magical time,
I was scared, like it was a passion,
To my storms, you were calming shore,

4 months and am counting after,
For a peaceful life,
Endless love, faith and endless laughter,
We are lovers from a life before.

14. I'll Help You

If I'm so terrible,
Then why'd you sing along,
You could have smiled,
And just let me pass the song,

I'm one for miracles,
So I smile and face the storm,
You stand there musing,
'bout my superhuman form,

And I know you wonder,
Wonder how it could be,

And I'm just hanging in there,
A little longer,
Just trying to be strong,

I'll help you get through all of it,
Broken heart, empty days,
Insomnia and fits of rage,
Crying isn't weak,
So get out of the cage,

And when you doubt yourself,
Just listen to this song,

If I‘m so terrible,
Then why'd you sing along,
You could have smiled,
And just let me pass the song,

I'm one for miracles,
So I smile and face the storm,
You stand there musing,
‘bout my superhuman form,

And I know you wonder,
Wonder how it could be..

And I'm just hanging in there,
A little longer,
Just trying to be strong,

I'll help you get through all of it,
Painful scars, guilty phase,
In your head a mindless maze,
Crying isn't weak,
So get out of the cage,

And when you doubt yourself,
Just listen to this song.
Just listen to this song.

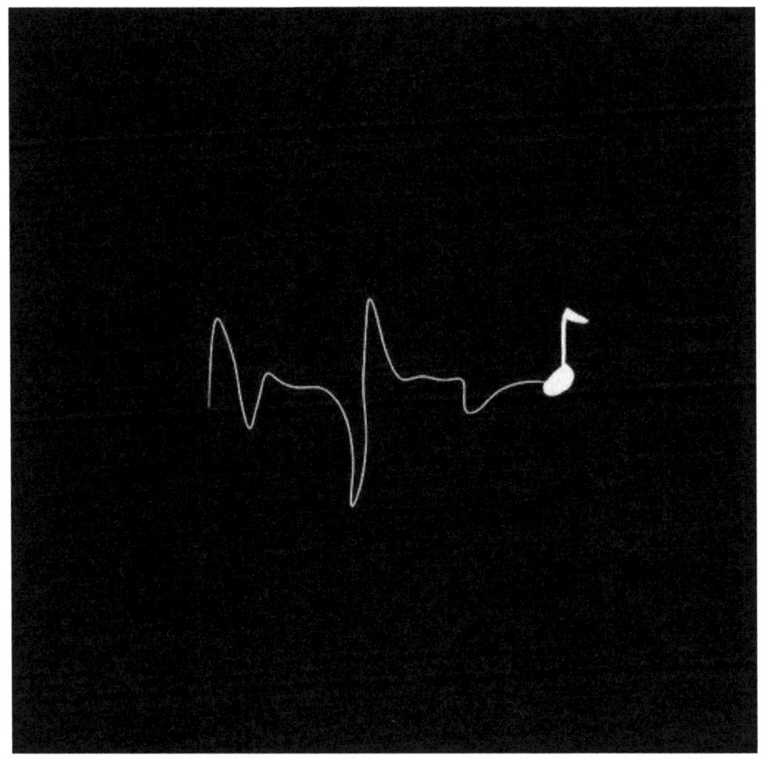

15. Limerick Love

The way he can see your naked soul through a cover,
Now that, little girl, is the beauty of a lover,
He loves no one else than you,
His love is no 'deja vu',
He loves you such, loves you with no less than manoeuvre.

16. Looked Upon By The Stars

Sick of the solitude,
Body aching everywhere,
My positive attitude,
Fading without your care,

And I'm walking on the rooftop,
Scared and in pain,
But this cold breeze is soothing,
My mind stuck on a negative chain,

Oh you're being missed,
But hey you're so far,
So I'm dreaming 'bout getting kissed,
Looked upon by the stars,

Come home to me,
Come hold my hand,
Come admire my eyes,
Cause shivering here I stand,

And I wish I knew magic,
Would've cast a spell,
And disappears all tragic,
As I breath in your smell,

Lavender you're wearing,
White lilies in your hair,
If you saw me tearing,
You'd hug me with all care,

So come home to me,
Come hold my hand,
Come admire my eyes,
Cause shivering here I stand..

And ohhh you're being remembered,
But hey you're asleep,
So I'm letting my heart be tender,
Looked upon by the stars,
So I'm dreaming 'bout getting kissed,
Looked upon by the stars.

17. Cosmic Her

A galaxy in her eyes,
The world becomes a bit more energetic,
When she dances and the world becomes static,
A perfectly aligned cosmos,
So calm, so serene,
A Siren for the chaos to come,
A ring of dust and fire,
Circling her vulnerability,
Keeping her intact,
Sparkling like glitter,
A mild shock to the touch,
A dynamic equilibrium for the soul,
As unstable as life,
As stable as death,
She who speaks for what she believes,
She who knows silence is worth as well,
A tiresome past she carries,
But she still hopes good and tries,
An aura of love,
A million positive vibes,
A part filled with dark matter,
Some negativity buries inside,
She is,
As the world calls it balanced,
Yet she makes an evident difference,

She is yet known as a human,
But she is more,
There cannot be perfection in the results we get,
But we can in the way of life,
She... She is imperfect,
But she is real,
She is who she is,
The world is a much much better place,
Because she is Amazing,
You are amazing,
I think we both are.

18. Night Full Of Stars

And yet another night full of stars,
When mine is standing in my arms,
She lingers on me with hands around my neck,
A gentle shy smile on her face,
Her rosy perfume and strawberry lips,
My hands around her waist, clutching her hips,

"Close your eyes", I whisper,
Excited, she giggles and follows,
Let's take away your hollows,
Let there be no more sorrows,

Let me be by your side,
I'll hold you close,
You just look in my eyes,
I'll make a move,
There goes a love song,
I'll get up and groove,
Groove with you,

Girl you're fire,
Full of desire,
Melting smile yeah,
Heart of sapphire,

Girl you're a day dream,
I've got some nightmares,
Lemme say I love you,
As the pretty night stares,
Stares deep at us,

And yet another night full of stars,
When mine is standing in my arms,
She lingers on me with hands around my neck,
A gentle shy smile on her face,
Her crazy attitude, she's roasting me on my face,
I put my lips on hers, so she could taste,

"Hold my hands", I whisper,
Surprised, she holds them tight,
Just like a guiding light,
Making my life alright,

Let me be by your side,
I'll hold you close,
You just look in my eyes,
I'll make a move,
There goes a love song,
I'll get up and groove,
Groove with you,

Girl you're perfect,
With no defect,
Oh you're precious,

Priceless in fact,

Girl you're a day dream,
I've got some nightmares,
Lemme say I love you,
As the pretty night stares.

19. Adulting

I used to be little,
Without any worry,
Then I grew up,
And here I am,

My body was brittle,
Now I'm in a scurry,
Now when I spew up,
Alone I stand,

Adulting, they call it,
Maybe I understand,

Threw tantrums for a toy car,
Now I save as much as I can,
Used to have a lot of friends,
Now I reconsider when I choose them,

Used to wait for my dad,
As he came back from work,
Then cried cause he forgot my ice cream,
He used to be tired, now I understand,

To grow old,
Is not to be an adult,

To be responsible and considerate,
That's now vogue to the cult,

To be an adult,
Is to not be just a woman or man,
To know who you are,
"I am who I tend to be and I can",

Adulting,
Is to make a choice,
To have thoughts and a mindset,
To know you have a voice,

Adulting,
Is to learn independence is a solace,
It has its own troubles,
But life, alone, you may need to face.

20. Love And Lust

Love and lust,
Companions in crime,
One seems good, the other seems bad,
It's all about making them rhyme,

Those crystal eyes full of charm,
They too send seductive shivers of lust in swarms,
Ears once decorated with the earrings,
Become sensitive corners of dominance,
Narrow neck with the Adam bulging,
Carries a sudden strong fragrance,
Hair he pushed back from her face,
He grabs them pulling her close,
Lips that seemed so delicate,
Are then clutched and bit as she rises on her toes,

In a moment, their bodies sway in rhythm,
Turning him around, loving him as much she'd desire,
Switching roles, cupping her sacred temples of sin,
Loving her soft as a petal, hard as a sapphire,
Getting down to the bulge on his lower,
Reaching for the ocean amidst her legs,
At times teasing, tickling, getting slower,
At times one does the master, one worships and begs,
On their knees, flickering tongues do the magic,

For moments they just love, forget about all the tragic,

Her equipped lips drip on the tip,
His firm hands pull her strands,
With moans and groans in the lusty silence,
Inside her heaven, tremendous hell he slip.

All this cliché,
What's sex when its easy to handle,
Blindfolded and bound,
Spank her with her sandals,
Stop resisting,
Endure the pain and the pleasure,
Show him your strength,
Make his balls bleed with the pressure,

Hungry kisses all over,
Rough traps to the wall,
Soon when the majestic moaning fades,
And the rises and falls simmer,
Laughter echoes in the otherwise silent hall,

Legs wrapped,
Bodies glued,
Warm kisses on the forehead,
They sleep so close as if sewed,

Waking up with the first ray of sun,
Looking each other in the eyes

An 'I Love You' leaves the lips,
After all the nasty fun,

Love becomes lust,
Libido turns into love,
Its all about making them rhyme.

21. Infinite In Me

Infinity you may use,
A word of mere eight,
There's infinite in it,
Such deep is it's fate,
There is none in nothingness,
An infinite of none,
Where there is infinite,
There can never be none,

You, me, this world,
Mere parts of this universe,
Known to us is mere one of a multiverse,
There is infinite in me,
There is infinite in you,
There may be infinities infinite,
There's only one you,

So live this life limited,
Survive this sacred survival,
Enjoy this enriching existence,
Rejoice even with your rivals,
Cause cursed is this creation,
And doomed is not death,
So find freedom from fright,
Bring beauty from your breath,

There's infinite in me,
And hence I shall live,
A life finite,
But an infinite in it.
Cause this is not the end,
There's more to me,
My existence is finite,
My purpose infinite,
There's infinite in me,
And I'm infinite.

About The Author

Hello! I am no more than a fellow human and yet I have a lot to share. I started writing from a young age and I write about anything that can pause my mind, be it a gaze full of love, a moonlit face or the struggles of the world. Love, hate, good, bad, right, wrong, all these emotions make me wonder about the enormous perspectives that can exist and I wish to understand as well as portray as many of them as possible through my works and at the same time hopee to bring about some change in this world.

Enter Caption

9 798886 670592

Printed by Libri Plureos GmbH in Hamburg,
Germany